Unburied Alleluias

I0833838

Unburied Alleluias

— Liturgical Longings from the Spiral's Edge —

Jill Y. Crainshaw

RESOURCE *Publications* • Eugene, Oregon

UNBURIED ALLELUIAS
Liturgical Longings from the Spiral's Edge

Copyright © 2026 Jill Y. Crainshaw. All rights reserved. Except for brief quotations in critical publications or reviews, no part of this book may be reproduced in any manner without prior written permission from the publisher. Write: Permissions, Wipf and Stock Publishers, 199 W. 8th Ave., Suite 3, Eugene, OR 97401.

Resource Publications
An Imprint of Wipf and Stock Publishers
199 W. 8th Ave., Suite 3
Eugene, OR 97401

www.wipfandstock.com

PAPERBACK ISBN: 979-8-3852-6883-2
HARDCOVER ISBN: 979-8-3852-6884-9
EBOOK ISBN: 979-8-3852-6885-6

VERSION NUMBER 02/13/26

For my Wake Divinity students,
who trusted me with their stories—
with what was broken, becoming, and brave.
Your wisdom and your journeys
sing through these unburied alleluias.

Author's Meanderings

These liturgical life-lyrics move through sacred time as cardinals, bumblebees, and moths fly. Delighting in leaves, bugs, and nests along the path, the poems spiral. They slip between forms. Some pause to breathe or ponder. Some sing sideways. Others linger. Some vanish mid-wing.

Why?

Because unexpected holy relics await us everywhere. Sometimes glinting in a summer sun, other times peering out from camouflaged hiding places, sacred wisdom lives in dust and dishwater, spider webs and sourdough bread. Yes, angels in starlit heavens sing boisterous alleluias in advent stories. *And* God-with-us whispers into our lives in hospital waiting rooms and backyard thunderstorms.

This collection listens for Advent, Christmas, Epiphany, Lent, and Easter by meandering. Advent peeks out from the deepening shadows of Lent. Epiphanies sprinkle their insights at noon. Resurrections come too soon. We are still waiting on others.

This collection's odes, psalms, and laments stretch our liturgical imaginations.

They are breaths and fragments.

They disrupt what's expected—because holiness rarely walks a straight line. Many bodies and spirits, including mine, have never fit the liturgical calendar neatly. So, I imagine here a calendar that spirals like I do.

You'll notice a spiral symbol marking certain pages. These pieces are meant as fissures and pauses—pantoum-tinged breaths, sacramental turnings, and invitations to reorient before the next holy wandering. Let them guide you like wanderers' way markers or cosmic breadcrumbs.

The collection begins with Ordinary Time, though, like a ruby-throated hummingbird, you may dance from one page or section to another to find your own sweet, nourishing nectar.

Thank you for meandering with me.

Jill

spiral's edge

they peer through ancient windows
humming old hymns in unheard keys

some say
they danced
on life's cosmic edges before
flesh
took its first breath

sacrament in a honeysuckle lamp

summertime nectar magic sweetening a
vermillion-bloomed
honeysuckle lamp

moscato mysteries
sweetening a glass thimble
at sunday's sacred meal in
the lutheran church
with the red door

mama's daddy
(i am his spitting image mama said) was
buried out back long before i sat with
mrs hartwell and my own daddy
on the very last pew
watching mama's curly-permed head
bounce and sway as she tap-danced
handel's water music
on ancient pipe organ pedals

my spit-shined mary janes kept time
tapping the spirited air above the
hardwood floor while I waited
for daddy to come back
from the enchanted table where the
magical potion he drank
from a tiny cup
made him smell funny
when i tugged his sleeve

i was grown up enough i was sure
        (i could read chapter books and
        ride without training wheels)
to taste those sweet solemn secrets
enlivened by tall waxy candlesticks
and light caught
in a stained-glass window
given "back when"
in memory of grandpa
who's waiting
in the cemetery out back
for grandma to come home

and that easter i did—
sip from the bloom of mystery
and the single tangy violet drop
stained my lips with memories

i taste it still as if for
the first time

summertime nectar magic in a
honeysuckle lamp

threads, webs, wonder

(ordinary time)

a flash of cardinal red
a-lights
great-grandpa's tombstone

(1905-1987)

ordinary time

hungry chicks

nest nearby

We Cannot Live Without It

Bread.

Golden-crusted loaves
seasoned by
the smell of the earth
passed from me
to you
to a stranger.

Bread—

that remembers the baker-
woman's hands the
farmer's tired feet
the child's empty table

We cannot live without it—

Wine.

Poetry bottled and decanted.
Kiss of sweet grace
on thirsty lips.

Wine—

that remembers
the taste of
blood-soaked earth—
Spilled out
between us,
for us,
you
and me
and a stranger.

We cannot live without it—

Water.

Trickling.
Surging.
Moaning.

Water.

that remembers
The Middle Passage.
Flint.
Gaza.

We cannot live without it—

Bread. Wine. Water.

The earth.

Broken.
Poured out.

Remembering
that does not forget
hungry, wilderness people
in neighborhoods, towns, cities.

Bread. Wine. Water.

Our hands—
baking, pouring, washing—
gifts of God for the people of God.

We cannot live without it—

bullfrog standup bass-cat

thumps and thrums

in the backyard brine

amorous onomatapeia

breaking through the rain

bluesy love ballad

spawning new life

Spun

We sat in a circle,
caught in each other's gaze.
Heather, hazel, azure, amber, emerald—a
shimmering rainbow of
regard.

Promises and doubts
care woven with mirth,
arcing across human geometry.

Then
stories.

Spun like spider silk
limb to limb
soul to soul.

Fine filament,
dreams clinging like dew—

We spoke some aloud.
Secreted others
until the spectral incense
that invaded us
wisped away.

But the web lingers still
to catch us unawares
when a door opens
and light kisses
forgotten gossamer threads and
bits of cobwebbed stories
shimmer
from that time
when we sat in a circle caught
in each other's gaze.

empty tombs

echo

wombs

Webs and Cocoons

Sunlight slips off silken threads,
spirals out from antennaed arachnids.
Radiant wings stir.
Tremble. Tear.
Bound. Becoming.

Webs and cocoons.
Cocoons and webs.
Warp and weft.
Death and life. Life and death.

We spin. We weave.
We enfold. Unfold.

Sacred filaments
crisscrossing space and time,
sacred shimmer stretched across
the old church beams.

echoing tombs

infants cooing

full moon hauntings

dusty dreaming dance

a spiraling

coming-out salsa

The Scarf, the Wind, and the Moon

No one knew where she came from—
sprung from the soil of her daddy's farm?
Blew in with gran's rose perfume?
Tumbled out of a thunderstorm, more likely.

We scattered her ashes
in the bluebonnet patch by the pond
guided by lanterns of summer fireflies.

She'd left instructions in her will—well—
scribbled on a napkin from the downtown café.
Classic her. Elusive
Fleet-footed. Always just passing through.

No one expected dancing winds
but just as we let her go,
a breeze caught a puff of silver-white
and flung it into
my face,
my lashes.

"Maybe she'll grow back now
that we've planted her,"
my sister laughed.

We knew who had the last laugh—
She'd always coaxed ghosts from frozen ground.

I wore her red silk scarf that day—
to keep her close, wrapped
in her raspberry and vinegar essence.

Now she—the rootless one—
seasons my hair,
tickles my nose,
and I laugh into the wind
as a waning moon climbs the trees

Architecture Repurposed

You find an old house, in the middle
of the road, in the rain
Water-soaked and out of place
Your eyes dart: here, there, here again

You take it—well just a piece. Who
will even notice the diminishment of
an old house,
in the rain and out of place?

The next day, you return just to
see who's standing watch
But no one minds—
even though the returning sun
catches drops of leftover rain
and sets them afire with light

So you dare
to snag another piece

And the next day another.

A lease, perhaps, on a new place:
Architecture repurposed, borrowed and worn
until all that remains
is a sacramental sliver

On that last day, you dance away
into the camellia tree by the deck, where
the terrier comes and goes without even
noticing
the new house you've been fashioning—
from an old house
abandoned
in the middle of the road
in the rain.

A Blessing for Last Year's Pecan

We usually chase time,
slipping through
the hourglass
        sands
                sliding
                        beneath hurry-up feet.
Now—
                each frame

        deliberate.

We hug our lives
        from dust
                returning to dust

        two cardinals meet talk
                        dance

        measure each other, then marry
        their lives
        in a berry-blushing holly

                        while bumblebees

                        samba

                        mid-air

until sunset when a full pink
moon perches for the night

in the crook of the maple with a
squirrel giving thanks
for last year's pecan

So—we pause too
and breathe
a prayer

they compost the hymns that
left them out

seeding life
into bruised soil

Compline

a beagle a terrier and their human wander out
under the stars
a circadian backyard

compline

to end
this day God
grant us restful

sleep

in heavenly peace
children of midnight mamas
who through uncertain times keep

vigil

i lift my eyes to the sparkling expanse out there somewhere a
teenager struggles to stay afloat
in a refugee sea while

dusk

falls into troubled dreams of a night-falling assault in
an alleyway behind a trash bin
a heroic rescuer

weeping

to remember what now forever stalks her heart
his too
lives changed in an instant

in the twinkling

of an eye turned heavenward
a beagle a terrier and their human
say goodbye to another night

a crescent moon

catches

a falling

star

rocks it to sleep

as morning sings

another advent aria

wonder, wait, pause

(advent)

a star flares

splinters the indigo sky

Flame-Dancer

Night spills sable
across the path.
Lost—we panic,
fear-frozen in place.

But—
We are not alone.

The lightkeeper
ignites a lamp—
a solitary fire-dancer
captures our eyes,
grabs our hands, pulls
us toward
her glowing stage.

We exhale.
Winter-solstice moths
Spiraling home.

Come,
let us dance
in Advent's light.

Toward the Fire

Bright flames flicker
somewhere down the path.
Wintry hearts go still,
ache for warmth—

For now,
one candle.
A single spark
to coax us forward
until the fire grows bold.

God of Ash and Dust,
Breathe into us, spirit-
air enough
to rouse the embers
we thought too cold
for fiery freedom.

Send flinty-flashes—
torch-glows of insight
to cast light on our
stumbling search
for what we dare
call truth.

Widen our heart-eyes
to recognize wisdom and beauty
still cloaked in shadows
of our tight-gripped,
stingy-spirited candle-making.

We need two
three four
million flares.
A growing blaze
to burn away
hatred and fear.

Inflame our courage as
Advent's fire rises—magnifies,
provokes, ignites—
revolutionary peace on earth.

Advent Pause

—after T.S. Eliot, in the spirit of "The Four Quartets"

The shortest distance
between two points—

a straight line— begin
here.
end there.

But the straight way?
Not the only way.
For some, not even the best way—

Beginnings cradle
endings—
    first rains
    first daffodils
    a baby's borning cry

Endings womb beginnings—
    a break in the rain
    winter sunsets
    disrobed trees

This is Advent.

Even the sword must learn to
slice open hardened ground.

Lions and lambs cradle peace
between them.

Green sprigs grow out of
axe-worn roots.

Defiance-hued crocuses shoulder up
through wintry wilderness dirt—

This is Advent.

We begin at the end—
end at the beginning.

We wait. We wonder. We pause.

they tell the ancient story sideways:

mary runs into martha's arms
lured by longing
dancing together
on the promiscuous edge
of god-with-them

We Wait

We wait.
We sing our longing:

> "O come, O come Emmanuel,
> and ransom captive Israel."

Yes, during Advent, we wait.
We wait in hope,
or try to.

This waiting?
It cannot be passive.
Not now.
Not when all creation groans. War,
famine, fear—
Back-bending burdens.
We ache—

Come early, Jesus.
We cannot wait much longer
for hope
for healing
for God-with-us
to be born.

we wait (again)

> "Fear not, for I bring you good tidings."

But carols sung too soon
storm our doors.
So do headlines:
Bombs batter bodies.
Bullets silence singing.
We try to pray louder— and
even louder—

> "Crooked paths will be made straight; rough
> places smooth,"

Bygone Advent promises
whisper to aching ears—

> "The peace of God surpasses human understanding."

while a mama and her baby
down the street
rock out of control
life—death
despair—mercy
their hopeless lullaby

Creating One,
Stitch into your flesh again
these threadbare fear-not tidings.

Labor in us today.
Break the waters
of our resistance.
Birth from our fearful wombs
fiery-fierce faith.

Announce in the marrow of our bones
God.
With.
Us.

kindle a fire

in the unrequited pause

exhale hope

beloved enough

to embolden the flames

Fear Not

Advent.
Hymns of hope.
Tales of shape-shifting angels.
Stoke longings
older than stars.

But peace retreats into shadows.
Chilled by violence and uncertainty we
huddle around Advent's little fire,
desperate to thaw—
frozen hands, frozen hearts

Can a two-candle blaze
Chase away fear?
Draw in the wounded,
the wandering?

"Fear not."
Mary.
Joseph.
Shepherds on hillsides—

They heard the singing.
Do we?
"Be not afraid. I bring you good tidings—"

firelight canticle

two candles

flicker

a not-quite blaze

whispers in shadows

we see

almost

not-yet

singing-sounds

old as earth

new as sunbirth

star-pierce

ancient heavens

from
cerulean

skies

song-cinders fall

on silent tongues

and
we
sing

Flinty Joy

Joy

does not knock.

She arrives howling,

birth-blood-wrapped

in cattle-trough straw.

Hope's first Godsong

                a prophetic wail

                        cracking open

                                the womb of night.

womb, word, wonder

(Christmas)

wombs birth

wonder

anticipate

(empty)

tombs

we wait (still)

Midnight's Christmas Lullaby

Can you hear midnight? She is singing,
a lullaby of stillness, gently ringing.

Yes, midnight astonishes the earth—
a whisper-wind, a fiery-star, a beast-beheld birth.

Awaken your hearts. A new moonflower is blooming.
Do you hear midnight? She is crooning.

Within the manger, silence sighs.
A baby is sleeping. Peace draws nigh.

Will you hear midnight? She is calling.
Through the stillness, glorias falling.

We gather as one beneath midnight's soft light,
Birthing hope from the womb of this mid-winter night.

Cedars in Snowy Places

Winter.
Solstice.
Gyroscopic dance
Choreographed
by Earth's axial tilt.
Sun stands still
Longest night
shortest day
Yule
Midwinter
The land is vulnerable now,
sometimes covered by snowflakes
that have let go of something
somewhere
up there
and pirouetted down
down,
down
from the heavens
to enchant
rooftops
and leaning-over fences
and autumn-tarnished grass.
And while tulip bulbs repose
in unseen silence
beneath the austere earth,
cedars in snowy places
fragrance the cold air
with emerald wonder

(still) turning

light retreats

ancient kaleidoscope

turning—

middle-aged mothers

laughing children

sleeping infants

turning (again)—

even those

homesick for

last year's nests—

(still) turning)

all wintering

waiting

wondering

And She Brought Forth

(for the mothers of Flint, Michigan, 2015)

And she brought forth
her first-born child womb-
waters splashing
nine-month hope—
and fear
breaking open
pouring out—
endangered.

Profaned river waters
gushing out
bittered by rust and rot
lead-laced silence
swimming down
eroding canals;
hallowed souls
betrayed.

Thirsty,
we weep.

O come, O come, Emmanuel.

She brought forth her first-born child.

No Swaddling for This: Mary's Mourning Magnificat

Rachel wails.

God—

migrated

down

down

to earth

through a woman's

birth canal

her heartbeat

and God's

a pulsating liturgy-lullaby

birth-blood

flowing out

to grace-saturate

earth's grit

no sentimental swaddling clothes

to camouflage a Herod-haunted world

God-meets-Herod

in Ramah where

Rachel wails

for her manger-birthed babies

alive no more—

her heartbeat and God's

a pulsating liturgy-lament

We are Rachel

broken open

And God

With

Us.

We wail.

And wail.

And wail.

A liturgy—

still aching for a refrain.

gloria in excelsis

and suddenly glorias in excelsis deo are ripped apart
by soul-slashing shrieks of women for their babies'

flesh offered up on hellish altars of an evil spell
birthed in power-poisoned cradles of maniacal terror;

no salvation, not for the ones who bore holy
infants, tender and mild, in their wombs

awakening from no sleep in heavenly peace to a
nightmare of babies swaddled in unhallowed graveclothes.

no one, not even God-with-us, pulled their lifeless bodies
from senseless wreckage to breathe into them the breath of life.

O heart-attacked city, how still we see thee lie—
carol-saturated sanctuaries now shattered splinters and shards

and who can make a way in a manger from what remains?
wise ones, perhaps, who risk the rubble when dreams call them to

"Traverse afar!" guided by a hope-birthed burning eye of heaven.
decant your bitter perfume, and don't travel home by another way.

"Stay." adore by refusing to be comforted. drink deeply
of Rachel's tears and weep her baptismal river into desert-ed streets

as you fling your mourning song to the star-emptied sky
"the hopes and fears of all the years are met in thee tonight."

a question

"wonder,

where

are

you?"

an answer

december sun puddled on the sanctuary carpet.
splashing in the light, they swirled, twirled,
danced while people settled into empty pews.

child poet-prophets, eight years, five, only three,
they swayed, tender trees seeking, reaching,
spilling morning gold from their hands,

unrehearsed, as far as we knew, and unplanned
except perhaps by angels, if you believe in such things. we
heavy-footed grownups beheld them, wondering.

and they danced on, in the light,
in front of the remembrance table where
bread is broken, baptismal promises spoken and where

on that day? innocent joy
graced wilderness-weary waiting eyes
with a wreath of swirling, spinning stars.

the music stopped, and they scampered
away down the aisle. I rubbed my eyes—yes.
their feet left a trail of stardust.

the way was prepared.

Words Made Matter

Words.

Matter.

In us.

God's love
made skin and bones
muscle and marrow
hands and hearts
God's words.
Matter.
In us.

No more speeches or spin doctors,
debates or diatribes—no—
God's nouns and adjectives and verbs
made alive
welcoming
respecting
loving
incarnating belonging in us.

Words made matter,
planted in salvaged soil
reclaimed
restored
valued
savored
and saving
hope
in us.

christmas pilgrimage

winter weeps

wails

covers her tracks

as she races wild

down the beach

where an orange umbrella

presses

itself

flat against wood pilings to
let her pass—
mama and baby
sheltered once beneath that
pummeled parasol
to build
summertime sand palaces now
besieged by salty snow
that soaks into the tide
and drifts
away—

and all the while celestial

diadems cocoon within

storm-expectant clouds

not ready to
blossom forth so that she might
gather their astral blooms to light
her winterward way—

mama presses
into the gale anyway
cradling her child while
one hand clasps to her head the
purple hat she had hoped might
defend against the howling cold but
instead threatens to escape
wind-flung into night
chasing
sandcastle-fragile
stars—

wonder empties her pockets

(christmas morning)

The Bells Know Things

The bells nod
As tower-hands of time
reach for each other

The bells nod
They know things

Sad
Things

Joyous
Dying

Birthing

Things

Hands touch
And the wizened bells speak
They perfume uncertain air with

Longing
Lamenting

Quaking
Calling
Clanging

Clashing

Tintinnabulating

Telling
Knelling

Glorias falling

The bells toll
And we weary wanderers
Cradle into their

Swinging
Swaying

Swaying
Swinging

"Take us, please,
To another time."
They nod and leap up

To verdant corners of childhood dreams
And back home
To mythical meadows beyond summer sunsets
And back home
To distant stars
And back home

Swaying
Swinging

For a twinkling
We remember

Because they remember

When their tongues
Are quieted
Ancient whispering winds
Sustain the sonorous song
Long after the sound has faded

We reach for each other And
the bells nod.

threshold

a dawning sun
shushes nightingales trilling

we hear

sideways prophets
foretelling rainbow starshine

disclose, marvel, wander

(epiphany)

Home by Another Way

Star-watchers.
Eyes wide opened by
what they see—

in a backyard night sky,
"they traverse afar"
to investigate.

Then—eyes wide opened
by what they see—

re-routed, home by
another way.

Ah, the prophetic peculiarity
of epiphanies:
shepherds
cows and sheep and donkeys an
angel-touched teenager and a
dream-visited carpenter sky-
gazing Zorastrians
on camel's backs
tracing a celestial light-beam to
a distant place.

But what of the rest of the story?

Menacing messages
from palatial halls
innocents slaughtered
by hush-hushed orders,
a mama, a daddy,
baby hugged tight
fleeing
across blood-soaked
borderlands.

holy visits
visions
vistas detours and dancing stars
midnight border crossings
into unfamiliar backyards kindnesses
of strangers
children's cries
wailing lullabies
"Hush, little baby! Don't say a word"
somehow?

Heralded
by a brown-feathered barn-bird
whose morning trill
continues the song
of distant stars.

So galactic light-spheres align
yet again.
Sacred sun arises
burns away
the fog of unknowing

and eyes wide-opened
by what we see,

hope leaps in daylight wombs
and we labor once more
to birth
love
and hope.

bread

water

for this journey

we cannot live without them

shattered snow globes: flight into egypt

globe shattered
womb-water gushes out
mingles with sacrificed innocence
in war-wilderness streets

mama and daddy
smuggle their baby
across jagged borders

feet pierced by fractured pieces of
heart-pondered dreams
escape into broken reality

birth
half-remembered
ancestral blessings
beneath a slivered moon

water

desert oasis

we cannot journey without them

(ordinary epiphany)

Chasing Epiphanies (A Star and Two Planets)

I followed the Bethlehem star into 2020's longest night—
Or was it two mystical planets, politely distant?

Chasing epiphanies? Not so easy
in a Fiat 500 on I-40 in midwinter darkness—

I stopped on an overpass, Saturn and Jupiter
still circling. Star-crossed lovers not ready to touch.

They kept their distance on the cosmic dance floor,
not ready to light up the universe with solstice salsa swings.

They've waited many moons to tango again.
"Span the distance," I whispered.

Then I drove home, glad for tomorrow's midnight morning
mist to weep in the treetops sooner than it did the day before.

desert oasis

night sky shimmers

(another ordinary epiphany)

spiraling way prepared

night café

you sit in the night cafe
sipping lukewarm coffee
from a plain white ceramic mug
a half-eaten slaw mustard and chili
cheeseburger and three fries
on a use-chipped plate in front of you
i saw you there last midnight too
and the midnight before that

a neon sign out front beckons
"always open" except for the "o"
that blinks and blinks trying to
stay awake to the promise

what bruised dreams
tether you to this thrumming lull,
keep you forgetful
that coming-true visions are
nocturnal pollinators
drawn to blossoms
that reveal their mysteries
only to the weary
who still look to the stars between
sips
of lukewarm coffee

night sky shimmers

manna from memory

packing up crusts and tears for the journey

(epiphany's advent)

ordinary hope

some wander neon-lit roads
half-hoping
even artificial light
echoes starlight
and illumines the way
home

Magi Dialogue

"Come with me."
"Where?"
"Wherever the star takes us."

"What star?"
"The fierce one—"

"I never liked the graveyard shift.
"How will we stay awake?"
"When will we sleep? I need sleep."

"Come with me."
"Sure, why not? I think the star
has a playful streak, by the way."

(The camels bleat. The night glistens.)

They turn their eyes skyward—
Eager. Reluctant. Nonchalant.

Wisdom wizards follow foolish flight of fancy—
a cosmic planetary alignment
a sixth spirit-sense
a thousand lifetimes of longings"

"Stop looking back."

"I left—things—
lost—things—back there."

"What's lost waits up ahead."
"What's lost nips at our heels."

(*The forest sighs. The star still pulses.*)

The trees exhale them
into dawning light—
a barn wren stirs
from nighttime nesting

The whimsy-fierce star hesitates—

They do too.

Midnight morning trees breathe
an infant lullaby, music brighter
than light.

"Come with me."

when god-with-us calls queens instead of kings—some journeys bend toward becoming

we three queens

she turned her face
toward still another way

her star—
the one flitting
in and out
from behind the night-curtains
longing to be a queen

silenced seamstress
stitching with shining threads a
magical morphing
cosmic constellation

in her hands
she carries embers dusty
stigmata
to illumine each step

yes

she turns
body mind
spirit

and bends the way

we carry bread—broken

tears poured out—grace

for this journey—home

we cannot live without them

weep, wonder, wait

(lent)

dust

spirals

she blew in on lenten winds

(a pantoum in four parts)

I

she blew in on lenten winds
i think i'll stay awhile
be your muse until this thing ends
her left eye winked a suspicious smile

you plan to stay awhile?
she tossed an ancient tweed jacket on a chair
looked at me with a smile
pushed back her fedora, twirled her hair

i eyed the tweed lounging careless on the chair her
costume convinced me—almost
the faded fedora, the uncontained wisps of hair
who are you? i smiled—a suspicious host

though her costume convinced me—almost that
she harbored dubious ends
who are you? i smiled—a guarded host
when strangers blow in on lenten winds

II

today i harvest the tomatoes i prayed for yesterday
she's still here—says she's a poet but i am unsure no
pen or paper, not much to say
she just watches me, smiles—a quaint saboteur

she's still here—insists she's a poet but i am unsure what
are you writing? i'd like to know she just watches me,
smiles—a quaint saboteur
who arrived uninvited, interrupting my flow

tell me again, what are you writing? i am eager to know
it's not every day a poet moves into my space
arrives uninvited, interrupts my flow
wearing a faded fedora and a dubious smile on her face

no, i've never had a poet move into my space
tell me—how do i rhyme your presence away?
because you are here uninvited, interrupting my flow
while i harvest summer tomatoes i prayed for yesterday

III

the apple doesn't fall far from the tree
she waxed eloquent when i queried her work
i don't know what she meant—she's a shroud of mystery
and her presence here? a self-satisfied smirk

as she waxes eloquent when i query her work
which, if you must know, lacks reason and rhyme
and undermines her presence here, her self-satisfied smirk
what? is writing poetry considered a crime?

well, no—unless it lacks reason and rhyme
okay then—look at your hands, the lines in your face i'm
writing poetry right there and that can't be a crime
we need to mark the moment—we need to leave a trace

she's right—i see my hands, the lines in my face
a poem is emerging in the body of me
she's writing it down; is that such a crime
when we know that the apple falls close to the tree?

IV

she blew in on lenten winds brought with
her a threadbare refrain i never meant for
us to be forever friends
but telling her to go has been in vain

she just keeps repeating her threadbare refrain "you
are dust; to dust you shall return"
and asking her to go has been in vain
her tweed's still in the chair—no end to her sojourn

"we are dust; to dust we shall return"
she keeps saying—her eyes full of hope
just let me stay—expand my poetic sojourn
let's rhyme our way together out of this weary worn-out trope

she says it again—her eyes bright with hope
shining from beneath her fedora—her hope never ends
let's rhyme ourselves away from this hackneyed hopeless trope
and see where we can travel if we follow different winds

Dust Remembers

(Inspired by global dust events and Ezekiel 37)

I am dust; to dust I shall always return.
But don't assume as you disturb my rest

with your omnipotent kitchen broom that
I am mere debris to be swept up and away.

Remember. We are interfused, you
and I, suspended in each other,

vestigial particles of endless galaxies,
diminishing and becoming, deposited

but for a moment amid yesterday's dinner
crumbs and dog hair. Tomorrow?

I am cyclonic, demanding skeletal trees
to dance with me through dry valleys;

or I am breathed out by destructive
detonating demons only to settle, leaden,

on a sandal-sheathed foot severed
from the child who sat at grandma's

table while she cooked the evening meal.
But I am also the cadence of the soil, eternity

dug up in a spade and sown with ordinary
mystery. Still, don't assume I am magic either,

or that you are, except when in a distant
sun-soaked garden we tango with the departing

light and time's muted colors bend onto our
backs and we carry life across ancient seas

to fertilize the future. Remember. You are dust; to
dust you shall forever return.

Ashes Speak Light

Remember you are dust—

We gathered in the sanctuary,
spoke of earthy earthly matters,
went our separate ways,
brows cinder-smudged
back into our everyday days.

Dust to dust, ashes to ashes
yet in between a light divine can shine.

But we who can choose
dare not hurry with too-swift feet
from this unforgetting,
this manifest marking
of human identity
fragility
accountability.

Dust to dust, ashes to ashes yet in
between a light divine can shine.

No, we dare not
rub this mark of mortality
with too much ease
from furrowed foreheads,
not while still-warm ashes
singe sacred Dakotan soil,
not while somebody's son remains

planted in fallow ground waiting
for forgetting people to speak
aloud that
black lives matter,
not while some bodies run for
borders they cannot even see
because the other side
of nowhere is safe,
nowhere is home.

Remember.

dust whispers

ashes listen—

winds blow

through cracked memories

dust whispers

(weep, wonder, wait)

snowdrops on ash wednesday

she kissed my forehead at night when
the world was drowsy and
mrs. beasley and I were snuggled safe
down deep beneath cotton-cool sheets
and moon-yellow blanket
a lone snowdrop tickling my furrowed
bedtime brow
prophet of winter's death
a mother's tender-fierce
twilight touch marking me

her fingers that served our Sunday
in-remembrance bread brushed my
forehead
weightless as a feather
floating across my face
perhaps from a house
finch escaping the hiss of
a neighbor's big yellow tomcat
to dust you shall return

kiss mrs beasley too i demanded
and she always did but not without
a fuss since mrs beasley is a doll
and not real at all except
her berry blush lipstick left
a puckered seal and

i was reassured since i
could never see my own forehead
but mrs beasleys smudged face
held my eyes
until night danced with stardust

(still another ordinary journey)

holding your hand (in secret)

weary-wandering through

whisper-soaked ashes. . .

For We Who Are Alone Together

I sit alone together with the whip-poor-wills, watching
sunsetting shadows sneak across the front porch

where a bold squirrel has left her supper crumbs to
taunt my tiny terrier when she bounds out

the front door for tomorrow's morning walk—alone
together with our neighbor's eggshell poodle who answers

to Rainbow (why didn't I keep my promise
to learn the neighbor's name?) and presses

her furry body to the ground in timid joy
when she sees us, even if we are a street-crossing

distanced from her. I hear a trumpet—or is it a trombone—
muted but clear down the street—or it next door?

Hard to tell in these days of recorded taps rising
like virtual incense up over the dust to which

we all shall one day return alone together. I walk
down the street as the ancient dogwood, whose

pink-tipped blossoms are unfurling one more time
like a thousand miniature flags, keeps watch

by the front yard gate. The horn sounds clearer but
deeper—a trombone, for sure. Not Taps, then, bugling

another day's end. Jazz, perhaps? Rising
up to caress unlit stars as though they are Aladdin

lamps hiding unspent wishes? A door to the neighboring
church is cracked open, a tomb unsealed:

hark, the herald vibrates from unseen lips
as an owl in the loblolly pine responds—

alone

together

we go out—

and dust remembers

the way

Savoring Gethsemane Places

they went out to the place of olives

where wind-wearied trees
bear bitter-hard drupes—
flesh crushed, pressed, poured out
until savory, saving

balm for broken bodies
light for tenebrous tabernacles

"My soul is sorrowful unto death."

they went out to the place of olives

where fickle sleep
betrays with
beguiling lullabies

"Couldn't you keep watch"

they went out to the place of olives

where the (w)holy human one
whispers up through ancient branches

"Let this cup pass from me"

crushed, pressed, poured out
savory saving salve of gilead

"Your will be done.

power in the blood

aunt gertrude played the antique upright in church every sunday

sometimes by ear
sometimes the old-timey way
reading notes shaped like diamonds or triangles

but the hymn she cherished most
her fingers knew by heart

power in the blood
wonder-working power

as much as i loved to hear gospel favorites
spilling from Aunt Gertrude's fingers
blood hymns troubled my soul

too violent
too brutal

i knew even as a kid how
much life and hope
the old old story had bled out over the years
early that vicious sunday morning
shots rang out

precious blood
wonder-working blood

spilled out on the
dance floor
in the streets
spattering shoes
dancers
doctors
nurses
police officers
lovers
friends

as we gathered for church that day
several states away
in orlando they did it the old-timey way
by heart

for those too often discarded
discounted
disremembered
now dismembered

a mile-long vein opened up
friends and strangers
enfleshing care until a flood
of plasma
pulsated through the city
into wounded souls

and as my little group of worshipers
lined up at the communion table
to eat the bread
drink the cup
share the holy body
i remembered that old hymn
flowing out from
aunt gertrude's hands

and for the first time i heard it hint
the only truth it could
there is

power in the blood

Into Your Hands

God-with-us, into your hands
I commit my spirit.

A baby's first breath—
Into your hands

The enchantment of a summer sunrise—
Into your hands

A cancer diagnosis—
Into your hands

A kitchen broom sweeping away
yesterday's grief—
Into your hands

Nails, and hands that refused to strike—
Into your hands

Each breath we take—
and our weeping for those who still cry
"I can't breathe—"
Into your hands

Every murmur and moan
in the marrow of our bones—
Into your hands

Creation-Doula
who delivered from
the belly of the earth
dolphins and dandelions
marsupials and marigolds

Artist-Activist
who ripped open surging seas
to create a freedom way.

Breath-Giving One
who holds the breath of life—
we exhale with longing

Into your hands

yes—

dust remembers

fierce-flinty

soul-sparks

buried

in

burnt ashes

we hear

tomb, womb, wonder

(easter)

the sound

of a stone

rolling away

vigil

for the Great Night

as life is dawning

stardust swirls–timelessness spills into time
spirit winds breathe–soil awakens

"it is good."

the sea piles up in a heap
miriam-people drum and dance
freedom footprints press wet sand
at water's liberating edge

stardust swirls–settles on split sea paths
spirit winds breathe–ashes swirl up

feet seek peace
trace garden paths
beneath trembling fig leaves
cypress and cedar keep vigil

stardust swirls–seasons forest floors
spirit winds breathe–branches lean in to hear

"oh, dry bones, listen"

stardust swirls–glitters on weary feet
spirit winds breathe–dry bones rattle, sinews stretch

while it is still dark
between a rock and a hard place
earth trembles
stones scurry away

stardust returns–touches earth's aching skin
spirit winds breathe–hope splits open graves

"it is good"

stardust

breathes

night skies

murmur

dust

remembers

Ode to Resurrection

(for Gail R. O'Day)

while it is still dark

we squint to see the path

to see anything

how are we to
recognize
believe in
hope for
crocus alleluias
when winter's nomads
run wild through springtime's
gentle
greenings

while it is still dark

it is no easy matter to see—
recognize
believe in
finding last year's
easter egg burrowed deep
in winter's nest of
unremembered leaves

and yet—

"our time is not what defines the hour"

weary feet travel treacherous roads
tear-tired eyes peer into cavernous not-knowing
fearing death—
yearning for
irreverent light

while it is still dark

autumn's summer remembrances
cultivate seeds in wintry graves
while all creation groans

"our time is not what defines the hour"
so

while it is still dark

we keep on rising up i
n the half-light
get dressed for the day's work
and make our way
step by step
as best we can
seeking
hoping for
believing in
becoming

easter signs in wilderness
places

while it is still dark

the tomb-womb

sings

Unburied Alleluia

the womb-birthed

tomb-bursting

seed-sower

flings startling

hope-sparks

with wild abandon—

Alleluia!

come out

come out come
out wherever you
are

they hid among the gravestones

whispers
shushes
hiding
from one seeking
come out come out
wherever you are"
tulips and daffodils
buried
among winter tree roots
hiding from spring sun seeking
come out come
out wherever you
are

they found themselves
in the emergency room during
easter vigil
among starch-weary scrubs
hallways crammed with

wails
sobs

hushed up corner conversations

and yet

resurrection

seeking *ready*
or not here i
come

risus paschalis

(when dust laughs)

spring has ambushed winter,
and the dust of the earth is, yet again,
transfigured into laughter.

dust laughing? not here.
not in this world's graveyard of abandoned joys
where dead-ended dreams whisper—
violated ghosts among tombs of those
too-soon returned to the earth.

you just smile and sink your spade
into the sun-warmed sod, costly
corruptions composted,
turned,
turned

turned again

until dust recognizes dust.

then you wink,
just once,
and the remembered dust,
tantalized
by the tickle
of a new feast's
first thin blade,
laughs.

stardust seasons us

shimmer-queer circles

curling

unfurling

outward

spinning back

to peer over history's

crinkled edge

and then unfold across time

with each breath

each flash of butterfly wings

each blushing bouquet of roses

each rain-dance

and birth-cry—

and funeral prayer

curving

swerving

swirling

toward the next remembered-resurrected

edge

we join the dance

www.ingramcontent.com/pod-product-compliance
Lightning Source LLC
LaVergne TN
LVHW020638100826
845148LV00012B/2229
9798385268832